Pretense and Pain

The essence of the struggle between
outward appearances and. inner emotions

Aneesa. A

Contents

————•··•◆•··•————

Preface 5

Chapter 1: Introduction- The Double Life 7

Chapter 2: The Masks We Wear 11

Chapter 3: The Weight of Expectations 15

Chapter 4: Echoes of the Past 19

Chapter 5: Fractured Facades 23

Chapter 6: Hidden Tears 27

Chapter 7: Society's Gaze 31

Chapter 8: Family Ties and Tensions 35

Chapter 9: Unraveling the Truth 39

Chapter 10: Seeking Solace 43

Chapter 11: Embracing Vulnerability 47

Chapter 12: Conclusion- Beyond Pretense and Pain 51

Preface

————◆————

In the bustling theater of life, many of us have become adept performers, mastering the art of disguise. We navigate the world with practiced smiles, donning masks that reflect what society expects of us. To us and the outside world, we may seem to be perfect. However, behind these numerous disguises lies a tumultuous landscape of suppressed emotions, shattered dreams, and unspoken pain.

This pain is a result of pretense, a product of our inability to embrace our real selves and our vulnerabilities. This book, "Pretense and Pain," speaks to those who resonate with this dual existence, those who are broken yet bear a façade of strength. It's for the souls who, amidst the clamor of the world, yearn for solitude—not as an escape, but as a sanctuary. A place where the cacophony of external judgments fades, allowing one to confront their innermost fears and confront the rawness of their true self.

Herein lies a journey—a journey not of escape, but of embracing. Embracing the fractures, the vulnerabilities, and the profound solitude that often accompanies our most authentic moments. It's a call to rediscover the power in vulnerability and the liberation that comes with genuine self- acceptance.

As you turn these pages, may you find solace in the realization that you are not alone in your struggles. You will learn that embracing yourself despite vulnerabilities is much more rewarding than hiding behind a seemingly flawless mask. May this book serve as a compass, guiding you toward a place of genuine reflection, healing, and eventual reconciliation with the person behind the mask.

Welcome to "Pretense and Pain". Your journey to authenticity starts here.

Chapter 1:
Introduction- The Double Life
————•··•◆•··•————

"You're full of secrets, aren't you?"

- Rae Knightly, Ben Archer and the World Beyond

Have you ever felt that you are living two lives? For example, the way you act and behave outside your house may be completely different from what you're like when you're in your house. We tend to show our real nature when we're in an environment that is familiar and comfortable to us. And when we go outside of that environment, out into the world where everything is unpredictable, we tend to get a bit defensive, and sometimes, we may even pretend to be someone we're not.

Being defensive is not the only reason behind someone leading a double life. The expectations of society can often force you to be someone you're not. Let me give you an example. Imagine a child who is very artistic and likes playing music and writing songs. However, his parents expect him to become an engineer one day. One cannot become an engineer by creating music. So, if the child decides to honor his parents' expectations, he will have to give up doing what he likes. But this does not mean that he is entirely ready to give up his dream. He would still play music and write songs during his free time. That's who he really is. But when he's out in the world, he is learning to become an engineer even though he does not like it. His life now has two sides. And it was the society's (or more likely his parents') expectations that forced him to lead that double life.

Here is another example. This is probably something you're familiar with. Quite often in social media, you see people who seem to be living the dream. They share amazing photos of themselves, featuring the beautiful life they are living. But reality can be very different. Some of these people lead lives that are far from beautiful. They might be sad all the time because of job- related problems, school-related problems, and relationship issues. However, the life they showcase for others to see is entirely different. They put on a show for the sake of others' perception. They want to fool others into believing that they are different from reality. Why? It's because they want to paint themselves in a different light. And the beautiful life they show others may force others to lead double lives as well.

Have you read a book named "The Strange Case of Dr. Jekyll and Mr. Hyde" by the famous writer Robert Louis Stevenson? It's a story about a renowned and respected physician named Dr. Jekyll who transforms into a murdering psychopath named Mr. Hyde at night. The book discusses the hidden nature of man and what it is like to 'play a part'. This goes as far as dual personalities; an extreme case of leading double lives.

Some people consider that leading double lives makes things easier for them. However, it is clear that managing two different personas can be really stressful. It's like juggling so many things at once, struggling to keep everything moving at the same time without dropping one. When you try to maintain two lives at the same time, you can often end up hating yourself and doubting who you really are. Pretending only leads to pain. So, what you can do to avoid this pain and mental stress is to tear down the disguises you wear and embrace who you really are.

Chapter 2:
The Masks We Wear

————→••◆••←————

"If you want people to love you for who you are, take the mask off."

- Quetzal

Why do people wear masks? In the past couple of years, we wore masks to protect ourselves from the pandemic, or the harmful viruses that may attack us when we go outside. In theatres, actors wear masks to become a different character- the one the audience expects them to be. In masquerade balls, people wear masks to hide their identities.

People wear figurative masks in their everyday lives for similar reasons. They wear masks- or pretend to be someone they are not- to protect themselves from the outside world. They fear that others might hurt them if they show who they really are. Sometimes, people put on masks to pretend to be someone they are not, just like theatre actors do. They become the person the society expects them to be by playing a certain role. And just like how masquerade masks are used to hide real identity, in everyday life, some people wear masks to hide who they really are. They fear that others may not like them or treat them differently if they show their real selves.

Those who lead double lives often wear masks that mislead the people they interact with. Masks help them become different people- the people they wish they were. But in reality, masks hide your real self. And this can have dangerous consequences.

When you wear a mask, or play the role of someone you're not, the person who interacts with those who are close to you is not 'you' but a pretender. As a result, the people in your life may end up liking the pretender and not the real you. Why is it dangerous, you ask? Let me explain.

When someone likes your 'mask', you start to fear what would happen when you take off that mask. Would that person still like you the same way even without your mask? What if they come to hate your real self and prefer your pretense-self over you? When this happens, some people think that their only option is to keep wearing the mask, even if it tires them out completely. No one can keep wearing a mask all day. The longer you keep up the act, the more you feel suffocated. Your freedom becomes limited, and you start hating yourself for what you're becoming. Is keeping up an act worth all that?

I have some questions for you. Try your best to answer all these questions honestly.

- Do you feel like you're wearing a mask too? If so, why do you feel that way?

- What are the things that make your mask-wearing self different from your real self?

- What are the things that you think others like about your mask-wearing self?

- What are the things that you like about your real self?

- What characteristics do you think others would not like about your real self?

- Now think about whether those characteristics are really as bad as you think. Don't let society's norms hold you back. In the end, what really matters is *you.*

Chapter 3:
The Weight of Expectations

————————→···◆···←————————

"I'm not in this world to live up to your expectations and you're not in this world to live up to mine."

- Bruce Lee

When you're young and still looking for your place in society, expectations can be a real burden to carry. The truth is that the people around you had expectations of you even before you were born! They might have had expectations of what you would look like, your hair color, your eye color, and so many other things. And as you grow up, the expectations of others only get more complex. They eventually develop into who you will become when you grow up and the role you will play in society.

Expectations come from all around us and within ourselves as well. Quite often, the expectations that come from outside can significantly influence the expectations that come from within.

Even when those around you do not speak out loud about their expectations of you, you can still sense them. You can feel when you have impressed them and when you have disappointed them. If you take their responses too much to heart, eventually, your expectations of yourself will be shaped to suit the expectations of others.

Living up to one's expectations can be quite tiring, actually. There's no end to pleasing others' expectations of you. When you fulfill one expectation, they will bombard you with another one. In the end, you feel like you're running a race that you can never win. And when you keep trying to please others and live up to their expectations, you eventually become someone you're not.

This is because you could not identify the expectations you had for yourself. During the race, you have forgotten your own expectations and adopted others' expectations as your own. In the end, you have no idea what you want to become because you've already gone too far. So, you decide to go with the flow and become the person you have been forced to become. This, once again, results in you pretending to be someone you're not.

In reality, you do not owe anything to anyone. Your life is your own and you have the freedom to decide who you want to become. It's quite alright to change your expectations of yourself. But keep in mind that your expectations must always be true to yourself. They must not be forced upon you by anyone.

Question time! Let's see whether you know what everyone expects from you.

- What does your family expect from you? What do your friends expect from you?

- What do your teachers and mentors expect from you? What does the society expect from you?

- What are your expectations for yourself?

- Now think about what you would feel when you fulfill the expectations of each one of these groups. Would you feel as if you're fulfilling your own expectations? How well do others' expectations of you match with your own?

Remember, in the end, all that matters is whether you're living up to your own expectations.

Chapter 4:
Echoes of the Past

————◆————

"What is history? An echo of the past in the future; a reflex from the future on the past."

-Victor Hugo

Our past makes us who we are. As we grow older and older, we accumulate experience, and that experience plays a major role in the way we act and behave. Basically, we learn from our past and incorporate the things we learn, however subtle they may be, into our daily lives. We experience things, we make mistakes, we go through a rollercoaster of emotions, we learn, we overcome, and we move on.

But sometimes, our past experiences can adversely affect the way we act. There's an old saying, "The man who has been hurt by fire will flinch at the sight of a firefly". It means that some traumatic or bad things that have happened to you in the past can affect the way you live your life today. This is inevitable most of the time. Your past makes you who you are, after all. What you need to keep in mind is that you must not let your past control you. Consider it as a learning experience, not something that governs everything that you do.

In the most extreme cases, a hurtful past can make us turn away from who we are. When we consider ourselves broken because of a painful past, we might put up a façade in front of others to show them that we are not hurt. And when we keep doing this for a long time, we simply get used to it, burying the hurting self beneath layers and layers of pretense. It might work for some time, but eventually, the echoes of the past will become too much to bear. When that happens, the entire disguise will fall apart, exposing our broken and hurt selves that we have been hiding.

The right method to face a painful past is to not ignore it or 'sweep it under the rug'. When something bad happens, we have to address that issue and solve it. Hiding it will only make things worse in the future. So, talk to your loved ones about your painful past and come to terms with it. Do not try to escape from it by developing a whole other life for you. Even if you go on living that pretend-life, deep within you will always know that you're lying to yourself. So, when it's time, rip off that bandage and nurture your wounded self back to the perfect form.

Now, let's talk about your past.

- Do you have any bad experiences which are still haunting you to this day? How do those experiences make you feel?

- Do you feel like you're pretending that those things never happened?

- Who are the people you can talk to about your past? Who will listen to you and help you come to terms with what happened?

- Are you ready to learn from your past and move on? Then, you have taken the first step into making your past a learning experience.

Chapter 5:
Fractured Facades

———•··•◆··•·———

When did creating a flawless facade become a more vital goal than learning to love the person who lives inside your skin?

-Ellen Hopkins

Façade is defined as a deceptive outward appearance. People put on a façade when they fear what society thinks of their real selves. So, the façade they decide to put on is something that they consider ideal. One person can have more than one façade. For example, they may act one way in front of friends, another way in front of teachers, and a different way in front of family. However, when all these facades fall apart, the real self is exposed. How well would the others receive the real self when the person has been hiding behind a façade for a long time?

Fractured facades can lower a person's confidence significantly. This is because their confidence has been built up entirely on their façade, not their real self. And when the façade falls apart, they are left defenseless, not knowing what to do.

A façade can also be seen as a role a person acts out in order to hide or disguise a certain emotion. For example, if a child is being bullied at school, it can make them feel upset and ashamed of themselves. However, they may want to hide these negative emotions by pretending to be okay when they are at home with their family. This façade would also prevent the person from managing and handling their emotions. So, these explosive emotions accumulate over a long time without being addressed. A façade that is put up to avoid facing adverse emotions can crumble down on you at any time. This is because you're hiding all those negative emotions and feelings behind that façade, causing your real self to be overcome with unbearable stress. What would happen when you cannot bear it anymore? When the façade fractures, you will be the one most hurt by it.

Another downside of putting up facades is that the people who meet you would not get to know the real you. The person they learn to like or love will never be you but the personality that you have adopted when you're with them. When you constantly keep acting a role and putting on facades, how are you going to find out whether those people like your true self or not?

Sometimes, when your façade fractures and falls apart, the people who approached you because of it will leave, causing you to suffer in pain and a sense of loss. This is why it's always better to let others get to know your real self. The people you really need in your life are the ones who love your real self.

Celebrities often put on facades for the sake of society. This is why most celebrities are often unhappy and stressed. The life they pretend to live is not the life they actually live or want to live. And over a long time, maintaining that façade can stress you out and overburden you with unattended emotions.

- Do you feel like you're putting on a façade in front of others?

- If so, what are the characteristics about yourself that you wish to hide from others by using that façade?

- Do you think the people around you would like you less if you showed them your real self? Who are the people still staying with you when you expose your real self to them?

Chapter 6:
Hidden Tears

———————◆◆◆———————

"The hardest part is not when the tears begin to flow, but when you have to hide the tears with a smile."

- Nishan Panwar

Sometimes, when a tragic event occurs, we feel sad, scared, and even devastated. However, instead of expressing these emotions and getting them over with, some of us tend to hide those emotions away. One of the reasons for hiding our emotions is the fact that we want to look strong in front of others. We believe that crying or leaning on someone else for support is a sign of weakness. But this is not the case. Expressing your emotions and embracing them for what they are does not make you a 'crybaby' as you may have been led to believe. It actually shows that you are strong enough to face your emotions head-on.

We also tend to hide our emotions when we don't want others to worry about us. We think we might be bothering them by expressing what we feel. We worry whether we might be inconveniencing them in any way. But the truth is, those who really love you would never think of it as a bother. They will always be willing to listen to you if you would only share what you feel. If you decide to hide your sadness or suffering from others 'for now', keep in mind that it will keep building up and ultimately crash down on both you and the people you want to keep it from. There is always a right time and a place to express your emotions. That does not mean that you should hide your feelings forever. Take the closest and most suitable time to let it all out.

Just get it over with, so that you would not have anything to hide.

As we previously discussed, struggling to maintain outward appearances, putting up facades, and hiding behind masks can be very stressful. The main reason behind this is the emotions that continue to accumulate within you. As long as you keep pretending that you're okay for the sake of others, you are putting your mental health in danger.

You may have heard this before, but let me say it again: It's okay to cry. Keeping your emotions bottled inside is only going to make things worse. Do you know what happens when you shake a soda can and then suddenly open it? The soda comes gushing out uncontrollably. This is exactly what happens when you do not embrace your feelings and emotions. They will eventually burst out like a fountain in a way that you cannot control. So, find someone who will listen to you with patience.

- Was there an incident in your life where you felt that you had to hide your tears?

- Why did you feel like you had to hide your tears back then?

- Do you think something bad would have happened if you expressed what you felt?

- Would you have felt any easier if you cried to your heart's content back then?

- If you ever felt devastated, who are the people who would support you unconditionally? These people can be your support system.

- You can even use a journal to write down the things you feel. Just don't keep those explosive

- feelings and emotions to yourself. Write down the following things in your journal whenever a big emotion takes you over.

- What are the events that led up to your big emotion?

- What was the trigger that set you off?

- How did the big emotion make you feel?

- How did you react? Do you think you reacted in the right way? If not, how do you think you could have reacted?

- What is the ideal way (as you think) things should have gone? Who were the people who supported you?

- How do you feel now when you look back at the events?

Chapter 7:
Society's Gaze

————•··•◆•··•————

"If your joy is derived from what society thinks of you, you're always going to be disappointed."

- Madonna

The reason why most people start pretending to be someone else is because they care too much about what society thinks of them. If you're a people pleaser, you tend to do whatever you can to make others happy, even at the cost of your own happiness. What is it about society that makes us behave this way?

Whenever we interact with the society around us, we become aware that others are looking at us.

We feel that others are judging us based on the way we act, behave, and talk. And when we become too aware of society's gaze, we start feeling anxious and unsure of ourselves. These feelings of self-doubt may sometimes force us to act, behave, and talk in a way that's different from our real selves. These behaviors we adopt are often a reflection of how we think people want us to behave.

It's good that you want society to have a positive impression of you. However, if you're pretending to be someone you're not in order to gain society's approval, that's not good at all. For instance, it can be highly stressful to maintain your façade for a long time. You will be aware of each and every little action and double-think every word that comes out of your mouth. You will constantly be on alert, wondering whether you're acting in the 'right way'. And when you keep doing it, you will eventually face an identity crisis which can be really stressful. This means that you no longer have an idea of who you really are. You have lost your identity and adapted that of someone else. When that realization comes crashing in, it will already be too late to reverse what you have done.

So, what can you do about the society's gaze? The first thing you should know is that the society will be looking at you always. So, rather than putting on an act for their sake, why not be yourself? And if you think that some of your characteristics will be perceived negatively, you can work on fixing them. For example, if you get angry easily, you can work on your anger management techniques. And if you easily get nervous in front of others, you can work on overcoming your nervousness. This would also improve your personality in addition to letting you be yourself in front of others.

- Do you usually feel nervous or anxious when you're interacting with others?

- How do you usually handle that nervousness? Do you address it directly or hide behind a mask?

- Among your characteristics, what do you think the society would look down on?

- Are those characteristics really as bad as you think? If so, how do you plan to fix them? (For example, if you get angry easily, you can work on your anger management techniques.)

- What are your characteristics that people find attractive?

Chapter 8:
Family Ties and Tensions

————◆————

"Family is supposed to be our safe haven, but very often it is the place where we find the deepest heartaches."

- Iyanla Vanzant

Have you heard of the saying "Blood is thicker than water"? This implies that family relationships are often the most important and strongest of all relationships. Your family is with you since the moment you are born and your interactions with them are what affects your personality traits, goals, and dreams most of all during childhood. Of course, these may change as you grow up, but they always start with your family.

Some families are very supportive of what we want to do. They ask us what we want to do and support us in any way they can. This is a positive family relationship. The children get to keep their own personalities and chase after their own dreams. But then again, there are families that force their opinions on us and expect us to shape our lives in the way they want. When this happens, the children start developing double lives for the sake of their families. They pretend to be someone else ever since their childhood and eventually start believing that lie themselves. So, they would do everything their family tells them to do, believing that it is what they actually want. And when they grow up, they feel like imposters, living the life of someone else. They would feel unhappy and stressed all the time and it would already be too late to turn back.

Quite often, younger children find themselves being compared to their older siblings or cousins. When that happens, they start believing that they are inferior and try to be more like those older siblings or cousins. Eventually, they lose their real identity and get lost in a race that they cannot win which makes them feel discouraged. So, if you feel that you're being compared to someone else, understand that you do not have to be like them. You are a whole different person who has different strengths and weaknesses. Use them to your advantage to improve yourself. Never try to change yourself to fit someone's ideal.

There's one thing you should keep in mind. Our families want the best for us. That's why they picture a whole future of us and decide to make plans to take us there. They believe that we would be happy in that perfect future they have imagined for us. Sometimes, parents push expectations onto you based only on what they know. For example, a mother may want her daughter to pursue a certain career because they could not reach that dream. So, they try to live that dream through their child.

Despite their best intentions, our families may not be aware of what we actually want to do with our future. So, if you can talk to them and clearly explain where you picture yourself in the future, they will support you. All you have to do is talk and all they have to do is listen.

Sometimes, it can be difficult to make them understand that your plans are better than theirs. So, do your best to convince them why the future you imagine for yourself is the best future for you.

- What do you want to do when you grow up? What are your main dreams and ambitions?

- Picture yourself as a grown-up, doing what you're planning to do now. Is that grown-up happy or is he/she missing something?

- What do you think you should do today in order to make your grown-up self happy?

- Do you think your family agrees and supports what you want to do? If so, that's great! If not, it might be the right time to have a good heart-to-heart talk with your family.

Chapter 9:
Unraveling the Truth

————•••◆•••————

"When you stop living your life based on what others think of you real life begins. At that moment, you will finally see the door of self-acceptance opened."

- Shannon L. Alder

Now comes the most important question of all. If you're living a double life or a life of pretense, how do you get out of it? How do you discover your real self?

First, let us see the benefits of discovering your true self. When you know your core values and your authentic self, you will have a solid identity. You will no longer feel lost or think of yourself as an imposter. Identifying who you really are and what you want to do with yourself will help you identify your goals and dreams. The earlier in life you embrace your true self, the better.

This gives you time to fit into your real role in the world and fulfill your life's dreams.

Ultimately, discovering your true self will boost your self-aware-ness and confidence, helping you succeed no matter what you do.

Finding your real self can be a bit difficult if you have been living a lie for a long time. However, through certain experiences, we find out who we are. We have to listen to our inner voices and recognize what is right and what is wrong. Discovering your real self is like assembling pieces of a jigsaw puzzle. When the right part falls into the right place, a beautiful picture is uncovered.

First, be quiet and still for a moment and think about yourself. Reflect upon yourself and think about your actions and how they made you feel. Keeping a journal would help you find your real self. Meditation can also be helpful in calming down your inner demons and letting your true self shine through. Some-times, when you listen to your inner voice, negative self-talk can discourage you from your path. So, always evaluate your inner voice and think about whether the things it says are positive or negative. When negative thoughts start rising, put a stop to them by thinking empowering and affirmative thoughts.

Thinking about your values will help you determine who you really are. Sometimes, the person you want to be can be differ-ent from the person you are at the moment. If you change your values to become someone else, you are disregarding your true self. The longer you think about your values, the more you will understand your place in the world.

When you have time, take a piece of paper and write down your strengths and weaknesses. These things make you who you are. Weaknesses are not something to be ashamed of and hide. Instead of sweeping them under the rug, we should think about how to turn them into strengths.

Find out your passions. If you're not passionate about what you're doing, you're probably doing the wrong thing. You feel bored and upset about what you're doing when you're living a life of pretense. Doing something you feel passionate about will always make you feel good.

- It's time for a little self-evaluation!

- What do you think your core values are?

- What makes you 'you'?

- What are your strengths and weaknesses?

- How can you turn those weaknesses into strengths?

- What are the things that you're passionate about doing?

Chapter 10:
Seeking Solace

————•••◆••••————

"If the pace and the push, the noise and the crowds are getting to you, it's time to stop the nonsense and find a place of solace to refresh your spirit."

- Charles R. Swindoll

Discovering your real self can be a tough journey. Throughout that journey, you will be coming to terms with who you are and understanding what you want to become. You will also start recognizing your core values and your goals. You will evaluate yourself to find out your strengths and weaknesses. Ultimately, it will be a journey where you will have to face who you are and accept the truth. As you go through this journey, you will start questioning yourself more than once. You will have to accept harsh criticisms and see yourself for who you really are.

When all facades fall apart and you're laid bare, you might feel hurt and wounded. You will question your newfound identity and ask yourself what you have been doing all your life.

In short, it can be a harsh and difficult time for you. During this time, you will need to find solace in the things you love and the people you love. They can keep you strong and make you keep going even when you feel like giving up everything.

Some people find solace in meditation and mindfulness activities. If you're a calm and quiet person who likes spending time by yourself, this would be a good place of solace for you.

Getting in touch with your inner self can help you feel grounded as you try to discover your authentic self.

Lots of people find solace in meaningful relationships. Do not be afraid to lean on others for support. Your family members and friends can help you when you're going through an identity crisis. Speak to them about what you have on your mind. Share your emotional burdens with them. Their words and actions of comfort will not only soothe you but also help you get in touch with who you are.

Start keeping a journal. When you're embarking on a journey of self-discovery, a journal can be quite helpful in keeping track of your thoughts and emotions. Write down all your worries, fears, and moments of happiness in your journal. Also, remember to write down how you felt during different situations. Those raw emotions and feelings make us who we are. Ultimately, your journal will become a mirror that helps you see your real self because it keeps track of who you were during every important moment of your life.

When you're feeling conflicted, focusing on self-care will help you learn to love yourself. Lean into what you like to do and try to discover something you like about yourself every day. Do something positive for your real self that you're starting to discover. That way, you will not only take care of yourself but lay the foundation for your true self to grow when you have finally accepted it. Always keep in mind that your mental health is very important during this time of transition.

- Who are your most trusted friends and family members who will be able to support you and listen to you when you're struggling with discovering yourself?

- What are the things you usually do to take care of yourself? These can be exercising, reading, journaling, etc. What are the self-care practices that you are willing to try out?

Chapter 11:
Embracing Vulnerability

————————→•••◆•••←————————

"Vulnerability sounds like truth and feels like courage. Truth and courage aren't always comfortable, but they're never weakness."

- Brené Brown

As we previously discussed, most of the time, people lean into pretense when they are not comfortable being themselves around others. They try to showcase their strengths and hide their weaknesses. This is because they believe that society can hurt them when they expose their vulnerable side. So, they put up a façade and start acting like someone else to hide those vulnerabilities. However, vulnerability is not a weakness. If we learn how to embrace our vulnerability, it can become a tremendous source of strength for us.

Embracing your vulnerability means that you are accepting yourself for who you are, even with imperfections. When we let go of the pretense and start acknowledging ourselves, we cultivate self-awareness. Assessing our strengths and weaknesses helps us in our personal growth and self- improvement.

When we expose our vulnerability by being who we really are, we create an environment around us that supports positive relationships. Those who enter our lives and interact with us will now see us for who we are. In this way, our vulnerability will promote trust and understanding, enabling us to build positive relationships and develop a good support system around us. When we feel that those around us love us for who we are, we become more confident and comfortable around them.

When you're willing to embrace your vulnerabilities, you become strong enough to not hide from your failures. When you know that you're vulnerable, you allow yourself to make mistakes and learn from them, rather than trying to hide those flaws from others. It helps to develop a growth mindset which is very important for you to succeed in life.

When you're living in pretense, you tend to disregard opportunities for self-improvement. This is because you consider your pretense-self to be perfect and are not willing to change. However, when you embrace your vulnerability, you become more open to new ideas and change, enabling you to improve yourself as a person.

We humans have a strong dislike for being hurt and tend to protect ourselves. We put up defenses and start pretenses to keep ourselves from getting hurt. You need to understand that vulnerability is a human trait. Even a person who seems perfect is vulnerable. Still, letting your guard down and embracing your vulnerable side will help you grow and support the cultivation of positive relationships. So, give yourself space to become vulnerable. Remind yourself that you are human and that you are allowed to be yourself. No one in this world is perfect, so you do not have to be ashamed of your weaknesses. Be brave to embrace your true self. What do you think are your weaknesses?

How do you think society will act if you expose those weaknesses?

Let's try turning your weaknesses into strengths. Here is a small example:

- I take a lot of time to complete a task. However, I make sure that I do it right.

  Now you go ahead.

Chapter 12:
Conclusion- Beyond Pretense and Pain

———————◆———————

"Being your true self is the most effective formula for success there is."

- Danielle LaPorte

Sit back and take a deep breath. You have reached the end of the book. Are you any closer to discovering your true self? If so, congratulations!

Throughout the chapters of this book, we discussed what it is like to live a life of pretense and what happens when the façade falls apart. We also talked about the path to discovering your real self.

Living a false life is extremely tiring and stressful. When you keep doing it, you will eventually find yourself with no motivation to get through your day. Every moment will seem dull and boring to you. And when you put on a mask in front of others, you always have to live in fear. The relationships you build with others will be false because they were built with the mask, not with yourself. Ultimately, you will end up hating yourself and start doubting yourself at every turn.

Life is not all flowers and rainbows. When you live a false life, it's difficult to face the curveballs life throws in your face. As long as you refuse to look inside you and recognize your true self, you will feel like you're walking on shards of glass. Every step will hurt and the scars will last a long time.

However, if you're willing to let go of the pretense, your pain will come to an end. What's the point of maintaining a façade if you're unhappy at the end of the day? Listen to your emotions and feelings. They make you who you are and define you. So, instead of hiding your emotions and feelings behind a painted mask, put them out in the open. Face them and learn to grow.

Always believe that you have been put in this world for a reason. There is no one out there who is like you. You are a special existence, and no one else looks, thinks, and acts the way you do. Do not disgrace that special existence by trying to be someone you're not. Remember that no one is perfect. Our imperfections are what makes us human. Believe that the universe loves you just the way you are- imperfections and all. So, embrace yourself for who you are. You do not need to act for the sake of others. Others are privileged to be in your presence. The moment you let go of your pretenses and embrace your true self, you start the journey towards success.

I wish you all the best! Go and be your perfect self.

The End